All the Invi

Mandy Pannett

SPM Publications

London

SPM Publications, Unit 136, 113-115 George Lane, South Woodford, London E18 1AB.

First published in Great Britain by SPM Publications in November 2012.

ISBN 978-0-9568101-2-0

Designed by Nnorom Azuonye

Cover Art: © Olu Oguibe, "Prelude to Autumn Blues", 2011.

To the memory of my mother, **Phyllis Knott**, to whom I owe my lifelong joy in words.

ACKNOWLEDGMENTS

Versions of these poems have appeared in Agenda, Everyday Poets, SAND, Sentinel Champions, South West Review, Excel for Charity News Blog and in publications by the Poetry Kit, the Pre-Raphaelite Society, Poetry on the Lake and The Right Eyed Deer Press.

'Mottoes on Sundials' won 3rd prize in the Ted Walters Competition 2010

'The Kelp Days' won 1st prize in the Wirral Festival of Firsts 2011

'Best After Frost' was chosen as Poem of the Year 2011 by the Inter Board Poetry Community (IBPC)

'All the Invisibles' (title poem) was first published by South West Review 2011

'Artichokes and an Olive Grove' won 2nd prize in the Build Africa competition 2012. 'Titania's Wood' was also highly commended.

THANKS

Special thanks to Nnorom Azuonye and the Sentinel Poetry Movement group for making this collection possible. Also to the generous writers and editors who have taken the time to read and comment on my poetry.

As always, love and thanks for ongoing support and encouragement to my family and to all my friends including those in writing groups and forums.

Mandy Pannett lives in West Sussex with her family. A teacher for many years, she has worked with all ages and abilities including special needs children (her favourite). She now works freelance as a creative writing tutor and has run residential and day workshops across the country as well as working with many local groups.

Her poetry has been widely published, both internationally and in the U.K., in journals and small press publications and has also been translated into German and Romanian as part of the Poetry tREnD and Poetry pRO projects. On several occasions she has been a prize winner in national competitions and has judged poetry competitions herself for *Sentinel Literary Quarterly*, the Slipstream Poets, Excel for Charity and two online forums.

Three poetry collections have been published: *Bee Purple* and *Frost Hollow* (Oversteps Books) and *Allotments in the Orbital* (Searle Publishing) She has also produced *Boy's Story* - a CD of poetry and original music. All are available from the author.

She has twice been selecting editor for *South Magazine*, an associate editor for the ezine *Muscle and Blood* and is the poetry editor of *The Right Eyed Deer*.

Her novella *The Onion Stone* was published in 2011 by Pewter Rose Press.

CONTENTS

BEST AFTER FROST

Mysterious how the medlar ripens,
softens, rots like Camembert – inexorable
in its breakdown, this progress into mould.

A smutty fruit: Shakespearian – seaside picture-
postcard rude, designed to raise a belly
laugh with hints of bums and holes.

Blettir – the term for overripe, for this slimy
slurpy process – such an atmospheric word, so
French this aromatic feel of rainfall in Montmartre.

Rain and footfall; blood-red light: A tale where rain
was far-off drumming; louder, thundering, tumbril
wheels; a ripe and rotten group ...

or not of blood but garnet-red: a medlar jelly
sweet for Spring's return. So suck this flesh and luscious
rot: *Best after frost*, they say.

PSYCHOPOMP: A GUIDE

He has a spider's
running shoes, this sniper scuttling
to an edge across a maimed
and screeching grid of fire

Psychopomp: a name to kindle
ancient dread, to conjure up that fierce
Anubis, overseer of viscera, the weighing
scales, a mummy's gut. Or else Orion
with his clubs who drives the souls
of weary beasts from lonely hills
to fields of asphodel.

He keeps a target in his sight.
Takes in a breath, lets

out a part, holds in
the rest. Adjusts

the crosshairs
on his scope:

Impact.

Bits of light
like dragonflies
blown up

And yet
it has a pull to it, that pallid
field, that asphodel where nothing
more can ever happen, where the sun
burns out and seeps away in quietude;
somewhere with all emotion gone:
a shunt displaced.

High-whine keening in the city
under dust's ferocious sky.
The sniper's dead and stiffening:
a thin arachnid ghost.

TWO FOR ONE

Let's call him Thomas.
No reason for that except he will doubt
for the rest of his days. Give him an Alfa Romeo, one late night
and too many bitters, wisps of a fog to blear his vision,
a girl who alters his life.

Let's call her Shade
for so she appears, timid and slight in the gloom of a verge,
unlit by even the moon.

One soft thud and an underworld snatches her up.

Let's move the plot on: Thomas returns
from doing his Time. For tonight all horror's forgotten
for here is his wife full of kisses and hugs and a table that groans
with a feast. And in comes his son in a red soccer top and look,
it's his girl on the verge of her teens with her ears
new-pierced and gold hoops to show him ...

Thomas, hold on to this moment.
Something is there in the dark.

Something that knocks at the door.

The boy in his jersey, the girl with her hoops, race to undo it,
squabble and fumble, take off the chain, peer out
to see who is there.

Let's call it
Vengeance

or Two for One

Call it
Shade's dad with a gun.

A TRAVELLER FROM THE SHIP OF FOOLS EXPLORES DRY LAND ...

and finds the landscape biblical
in stone and desert, locusts
and dry heat.

Here a man will sell his birthright
for some lentil soup.

Elsewhere a preacher
conjures fish, transforms
the wedding wine.

*Our Traveller consumes the loaves, spits out crusts, disregards the
hungry-eyed ...*

blocks his ears to a saint who shouts:
'Get a knife and cut your throat!
Beware of Gluttony'

With demons in a hot pursuit our Traveller escapes ...

to a feast that's for status: lobsters, oysters,
an abundance of turtles –

He belches and finds himself in a ward ...

with a lady of size
who grins at a camera filming
her guts, stapled
to make her look thin.

This radical cure alarms our good friend ...

who's relieved when he hears
poor Man's not at fault – it's food
that's really to blame.

Close to obese he returns to the ship ...

where far below deck
chained up in the hold, are the starving,
the unwilling thin.

DISPERSAL

Huguenots moved into Deptford.
Like red ants scalded with water
they were on the run.

In the pitch and lurch of survival
they dug another Eden, stung any
who would crush them.

Later their descendants' children
sleepless on a Saturday night
listened

as winkles in the market
screamed
by the bucket-load

and bulldozers
in an angry high street
flattened its voltage and hum.

On a hot day after rain
the red ant mates
in high air

bites off her wings
to feed the offspring
makes a different nest.

SHE CAME TO HER WEDDING

with plentiful gifts, scavenged
from trade routes, squeezed from the rich.
There was haggling of course and many
sly digs but still they arrived from Cadiz
to Southampton: caskets and barges
of gilt and of emeralds, sovereigns that shone
like the glow of a vow in this dowry
fit for a queen

including (in small print) the red
sweet-potato: cart-loads abundantly
year after year. The husband, enamoured,
scoffed dozens each day of this gut-
swelling, succulent root

then roistered on homewards to do
what he must (for his taste in potatoes
outweighed a dull wife)

who'd rather count seeds
of the bright pomegranate – redder than beads
that she told on her rosary; redder
than menstrual blood.

Passion soon
shrivelled like small-sweet potatoes
roasted too long in a black charcoal bed. Later he'd try
to produce his own version with offers of prizes
for those who might help him to breed
in an Englishman's soil

which, without the constancy and cherishing of sun
was brutal-cold and never
would give yield.

TRUST THE SUN

You are high as a seagull on this cliff.
There's salt in the air and a motley of light.
This, you think, is what being dappled must mean.

Alone for once you've chance to put
yourself in pasture, trust the sun
to warm your harried world.

Yet you are uneasy
at leaving your men to swarm
in their disquiet. Gullible,
they'll fall for any tricks.

Remember what happened before?
Enticed by honey, transformed into beasts
with voices and bristles of swine -

how they wept in their pens at the losing
of this, their luscious world.

Now you must check the ship, the tides,
look for changes in the moon.
How long may a man
make his home on an island
anyway?

Your men complain their bellies
rumble, query why the sun god's
cows are still protected by decrees
that say their skins and horns
are sacred, owned
by no one here.

Look, the sky is sunless; white.
How cold the world would be
if Helios should shine among the dead.

Odysseus, there's flesh on fire, can't you
smell the roast, the raw, hear that cow lamenting
for her calf?

Cattle bellow on the spit:
a roar of pain that cleaves a rock.
The sun is plunging down.
Your island tips.

A BAYEUX HORSE SPEAKS

They tip the boat sideways
to make us step off, still with our sea legs
and bowels of blancmange and it's goodbye
to being lined up in the hull like clones
or flat-headed cartoons.

As we come stumbling out of the cloth
our eyeballs are whiter than fear.

A pause
for our hooves are tangled in threads:
russet and golden like apples and bees.
A young girl in blue hurries up
with cool water, soothes away
jitters and mess.

Arrows like blowflies crawl out of the frieze
zoom up and blacken the sky.

Ahead
are horizons of rage.

FOR LOVE OF A SEVERED HEAD

She is a glassworm
in a toxic stream

transparent and soon
crushed.

Hound with small ears
don't cringe and beg for help:

vulnerable,
she has none.

This is the hour
of fist and kick

dishes are filled
with motifs

of death, a hawk
rips a feather to shreds.

To each in the scene
a space.

Beyond the archway
waits the grave:

wortle-berries
fall on flint

a knife
cuts to the bone.

Weep on, Isabella;
there's never been a cure

for loving
a severed head

MAVERICK OF THE GREEN

He is no Johnny Appleseed, no digger
levelling out the land to re-
locate its grain and stock, no figure

who'd inspire a cause – Freedom
has a simpler face when wars
are small as weeds.

He's always liked the foraging
for wild and hidden foods: makes roux
of violets, primrose pasta, porridge

laced with purple berries, soups
and casseroles of nettles, artichokes
with stub-root carrots, scoops

of rhubarb, quince and comfrey, yolk
from barnyard eggs. Thistles, pignuts, maize
and sweetcorn, plants in cracks

by drystone walls, a hoard, a haze
of cuttings, snippets – every bit is harvested
in warmth of autumn days.

Time and seasons turn around: a winter light,
ill-fitting, loose. From the window of his flat
he gazes down on hammered earth, soil that's tight

and dry and locked, derelict in scattered
wastes of tin and rust and rock.
He tries his best to brighten up this rat-like

tattered space: carries tubers in his pocket –
like an under-cover spy he spreads
and buries them at night – mint and rocket,

parsley, chives, all camouflage as shreds
of grass; sunflower seeds and bulbs for spring
drop into meagre beds.

Now he becomes a saboteur, a maverick
against a mob that calls him crazy, out-of-date,
pansy-planter in a tip

an ageing hippie, dinosaur, a gullible luddite bait ...
Later he will eat an apple, plant the core beside
a verge, realise how cold it is, and late.

MOTTOES ON SUNDIALS

After darkness, light

Enough at first – starlight, sun

Sufficient, this halving
of time

Alas, how swift

Movements of shadows are witnessed
by notches and twigs

I wait whilst I move

It becomes a matter of turning of tides –
the wax and the wane marked out
as a circular
O

So passes life

'The sons of Aulus and of Lucius
built together at their own expense
a seat and a great sundial'

They are voids in the ash

Mottoes on sundials
are frail

'STOPPING A BUNGHOLE'

A man may sing of love but never
know it for himself, plot a murder yet
not lift a knife.

Who would claim experience is wisdom's only key?
A one who'd write of suicide and think
to try it first?

Too many niches are precise, uniform
in nook and alcove, sprites and threads of air
will drift away ...

Why talk of dreams as fancies lost?
This imagination game is no more arduous
than a doodle, only needs a cloud

with humps and we see camels or like Fools
recruiting elves we blink and find our sudden selves
aboard a stormy sea. Enticed to forms

of things unknown we trace the dust of Alexander
to its final stopping point – the bunghole
on a barrelful of beer.

DÜRER, IN AND OUT OF EDEN

Was he frightened, that hare, shut in a cage?
Did you soothe him, Dürer, stroke his long ears,
notice the trim of his fur, whiskers,
the texture of him?

Look – you've captured the window frame's
reflection in his eye.

Rodrigo has given my wife a small green parrot.
She has bought a washtub, bellows, a pair of slippers,
a cage for the parrot, jugs.

Like Adam you named and noted all things:
stivers for leather, ducats for mussels, buffalo horn and the hoof
of an elk, fir cones, velvet, the red of an Amsterdam brick...

A lover of detail you were obsessed with an ox's nose,
the huff of its breath.

I decided to learn dancing and went twice to the school,
for which I had to pay the master a ducat.
No one could get me to go there again.

No, dancing was never your style. Better by far to travel to Zeeland,
see the corpse of a stranded whale. Decayed and stinking
it was unsketchable – unlike the salted walrus head
you copied with scrupulous care. Fearful, the blades of its tusk.

The fire alarm sounded and six houses over by Peter Pender's are
burned and a cloth for which I paid yesterday eight ducats is burned,
so I too am in trouble.

You knew that earth strips bare to its roots:
drew cocksfoot, meadow grass, daisy and yarrow in chaos
and bleakness of turf...

I have seen the bones of the giant of Antwerp; his leg above his knee is
five and a half feet long and beyond measure heavy

... and you knew how to cut a skull into wood
with Death on his thin white horse.

italicised parts are from Dürer's journal

DAISIES FOR KEATS

How bad to be stifled by walls. To have lungs
with hooks that shred every breath and turn
each nerve on a spit. It hurts me to read
how you cover your face with your hands
and weep for a girl. That you wake distraught
finding yourself still alive. Who knows
what quickens my interest in you or why
I should care – there's sorrow enough
outside my door – or why I bring daisies
to lay on your grave and hope, deep down,
you're aware that I have and are glad
there is spring in the air. It's painful to think
you die like a mullet encased in glass
at a Roman feast when the midwinter sky
in your casement window is restless with light
and there's still so much you would do.

A NEW CARTOGRAPHY

It is dark by the river, by this bridge's
underbelly: struts intertwine, cross-hatch.
He feels insignificant; small: an ant
within a clod of grass.

The bridge is singing a cappella –
voices of women shift in its iron:
a Celtic lament of the lowlands,
drowning, an elegy, death.

He wears a bracelet-like device, for this
is a sentient city. A new cartography
measures his skin, the contours and spikes
of his nerves.

He wonders why the chart of him
should always be so flat: no troughs, no peaks, no
lines of joy – once he stopped to hear a song:
a blackbird in a tree. The graph recorded
gentle frills at this.

Let them keep it all, he thinks, their precious
watchtowers on a wrist. Let them analyse
the heart of man.

The bridge still croons its ballads out, its chords
of broken love. He thinks about the note
he's left and hopes it hurts her, hopes
she drowns in guilt.

'Now it's bound to peak,' he says.
A pigeon watches at the water's edge.

TRUE FLY

It has a chime, your latin tag, *musca domestica*:
a warm Italian feel like cool frascati wine.
You deserve to rest your wings, be a guest

with oranges, the silver-green of olive leaves, to dine
and walk on sugared almonds with no fear
of spider or of man. Other insects of your kin

may think, erroneously, they are your peers
because they share a syllable, the latter sliver
of your name: the dragon and the firefly are dear

to lovers, artists, poets who will give
a gape of time in single-minded quests
for beauty's gem. Yes, this is it: the pivot

and the crux. You, with your astounding eyes, are pest –
the Lord of Flies Beelzebub, maggot
in a corpse's rot revealing time of death. The rest

is overlooked and written off. Is this the gamut
of your life, a hopeless, dismal, summer moment
chance to co-exist? Against the white

you show as blot, a splat on concrete or on snow
with wings dark-veined, transparent, dull –
yet rainbow light, like oil on puddles, glows

within a darker frame: the quintessential, frail
part that is not swatted, zapped or flung
outside the door, the window glass, the pane.

Animals were kept in shelters in the age of iron.
True fly did you go after them to warmth and liquid dung?

GROUP OF EIGHT

In this rock and snow-
tipped whiteness, ancient
hills stretch out like deer who

alert to rhyme and myth, still yearn
to lead the sleighs and bells
across a cold-blue sky.

And in this season's essence too
the lowest orders of the gods
may swing their pride

of antlers high and whirl, un-
kettled in a swell
of bison, auroch, earth.

Now fingers drop upon the lock:
the skull, the claws, the empty
eyes of Watchers

in the grotto's heart; a patina
of un-cracked code
in spirals, lattice, dots.

There's ritual
in this hematite as symbols
pulse in clay –

In tallow dull
and shivering light, a group
of eight small hands.

THE HURT OF MAN

Backscatter with the speed
of thought to Nordic tales and one

for whom the lulling hours mean
curses in a stranger's tongue like stone

in frozen bread. A black and wolvish
world of ice, too thick at first

to shatter-cut while hurt of man
is seeding in the grass. Enough

to measure shadows with a twig
and cranberry notch, for time to turn around

the waning moon. Violating
silent girls he sees that those who plough

the viper fight for guts of fish. Now
a wolf devours the light as icebergs

cleave in Tuonela and he's lost
in acres of the crow.

WOLF'S GET

Begin with a riddle, my lord would say
those winter nights when I was his bard
and the mead-hall rang with my song:

> *A harbinger of early spring*
> *sometimes heard but seldom seen*
> *I sing my name.*

> *Abandoned by my closest kin*
> *I bear the blast of others' scorn*
> *the lightning-lash of rain.*

Now spear-men trap me in this fen
where flies with fretful-weary wings
lurk in a marsh-mire gloom.

Liars, all the ones who call me
outlaw, wolf's-get, thief:
they would kill my best of dreams
fell me at the forest's edge
allow the sea to sip my bone
clod me in dark earth.

I would have a sester of honey
snout of a plough to furrow my land
the fins of an anchor to hold me steady
in the dash and dazzle of waves.

Wait, my girl with plaited hair,
wait at dawn by Cyrtlan gate,
the deer pool next to Tuha's tree,
wait three days for me.

The *cuckoo* is the bird of spring
who cries his name in double notes
and warms his frost-breath winter quills
with candles of the sun ...

Now let Spring
that laughter-smith, bind

the eagle's claws in blossom
fill a basket with blue sky and tip it
down through heaven's leaves to drench
my roots, to sing, to bring me home.

THE STARLING POINT
(misreading of 'starting')

A summer-wind day and a word
misread that ushers in rune-stones
tilting like shadows to tell how a wolf
has swallowed the light for many who lie
far over the seas and one young
warrior dead in a port on his way
to fight for Canute ...

They only had minutes or less
in the shine and it's dark outside
of the bright stained-glass and here
is a plaque to Pepys and Mother Goose –
both buried deep in the nave.

So gloomy a point to a starling day:
think harps in the rain-hall, skies
as blue as fjords.

STUNTED

They say he lacks parental care.
He wonders if that means the day his mother shoved him
in the dustbin, kept him there with bricks
to stop the lid ...

A dark and raven world
with holes no sweets can fill.

He knows a rock upon the moors
that legend says was once a Troll.
He likes this stunted, Nordic creature,
gives it names and tells it jokes, sits down
beside its stony base to nurse
his welts and plot
more stealing, shelters
from the rain.

He has a penknife which he hones
upon this troll to make
the blade as sharp
as every curse.

LATER, ALL AT ONCE

Noon. Summer. 1326

He invites the neighbours to visit his window:
the valuable one, its angles of glass. She, so
busy with apple-garth fruits, sees how lead
soon thickens light as if it were dusk, as if
there was less than an hour till night.
Outside, grasses are parched.

Biblical, date unknown

The time of begetting. A tale of twins
who fight in the womb, parents who age, grow

ancient in tents, a red-headed rebel
who wrestles an angel, pillows his head

in a darkening field on a rock
by a long-dry well.

Autumn. 1934

Intrigued by a curve
he ambles around, discovers two
fever vans deep in the undergrowth, lost
since Boer War days.

She dusts one and gives it
a wash of white paint, calls it his studio, nobody
else may go in.

The other she colours sun-yellow:
a love-nest intended
for them.

Five hundred million years ago:

New York's below
deep-ancient seas. Such

names we have given them, those
cold seas: Iapetus, Baltica,
Laurentia –

Tales that will never
have a first time of telling
close in.

1600 BC The Levant. A beach, a man, a dog ...

... who digs among shingle, chewing
on snails, runs back to his master with livid-wet
jaws, purple as indigo rain ...

> *(1200 snails*
> *crushed in a vat*
> *will yield up drops*
> *of Tyrian purple;*
> *dye a garment's*
> *hem.)*

April 15 1802

'Some lay their heads,' she notes in her book,
'on stones as if they were beds.'

Later she sees
how daffodils
swell like a curve in the road.

AD 30 Dinner time. Rome

A mullet is not
fresh enough, he writes,
unless it dies by the banqueter's hand.

Enclosed in glass the wilting fish will flash

through flame and purple-red to shades
of stone and cream.

Guests sip wine in myrrhine cups
as all the scales change hue.

1940s   Bologna. Italy

He cleans off labels from vases and bottles
washes the glass in a white
thick paint, takes people
out of the view.

Now he can cherish the dull and the matt;
grasses that parch in a sun.

1170 BC

Dark the Cornish megaliths, all joy of living
gone. Ancient giants who fought
invaders, wrestled but
were overthrown, crushed
to shadows, into
leaden stone.

1480 Tower of London

Imprisoned as rebel he thinks
about war; imagines a rose-

tinted battle and quest, windows
in love-nests and copper-

hot dragons who drink
from the very last well.

Midnight London. 1843

smitten by blueprints
she dreams about algae
iron, potassium
salts

feverish hot in a dry
dark place she is restless
and tossing, hears
a voice crying
I only have half
of the charm ...

down in her dream
she is wild frond curving a shell

2009 August. A Country Fair.

A gabriel-gold low sky.

White cows in a pen
are fingertip soft.

August 1942 Iceland

Enamoured with the still-life of buoys and anchors, chains and wrecks,
he sketches a propeller that reminds him, he says, of a daffodil bloom.
Later he dreams of a gibbous moon and a sun together, side by side, in
a parched and coppery sky.

On his last but one mission he flies above mountains that stretch on for
miles: a lunar landscape pillowed with craters, pale as salt with
shadows like fronds in a pool. A barrage of dust is thickening light; he
is smitten by longing for rain.

July 31 2010 Cyberspace: The Twenty Billionth Tweet:

> ... ' that means the barrage might come back
> later, all at once.'

> 'Scary,' he says. 'What are the chances?
> Maybe I'm going to die.'

2010 Evening. Bosham. Sussex.

Pale light on pale land, mudflats and a few seabirds,
a shadow-wash of fish. Winds across the estuary
moan like grieving cows.

There is less than an hour till night.

EVERY LAST BELL

Falcons are nesting high on the Tate
as mud-diggers rummage for tokens and beads
and above them the bridge with its glittering vertebrae
    leads to a brutal-wide
        beautiful city

    and Milk Street flows
along River Island with cherubs and garlands and fire-
    white cracks and every last bell in sweet Picadilly
whips across Saint
    George Hill

    and we're through and across
in this early sun to where an old Market, scrubbed,
sluiced down, offers no hinting
    of fugitives
        swinging in bits

    as long shadows sink
under concrete and grit like lost city rivers, to silt
in a garden that's cordoned and sealed
    with a whiff of forensic, a small
    white tent ...

O falcons in your perilous tower
    how fiercely you gaze down
    upon this grid.

A FOSSIL'S CHIRP

I have heard them at dusk, those crickets,
and all through summers of wide open nights:
score upon score; each of them
a green violin.

Today, a fossil
has been unearthed from an ancient wood
and its musical parts –

plectrum and teeth on the fringe of its wings –
re-built and its chirp re-heard.

This is a call from Jurassic grass
love songs plucked from a primitive wind
a brief copulatory sigh.

A SEASON OF HANDS

There's more to these pages than radiant colours or letters
inscribed with a quill. Vellum keeps its prints of smells, the blood-let
of a goat or calf, lime and skin and grainy hair, gallnut, gum and wine

Narratives creep up and leap from gold designs of prophets,
clutch at me through jewelled patterns, clawing
out of hell

This will be the wild one: an artist with a tough-as-pumice
style of twisting thread, of sculpting rolls of muscles on a saint. Look
at fierce Elijah's eyes: he'd shred old Satan's nose

Here is one with gentler touch. The corpse's cerements are soft
and drape across a careful frame in pale and fragile flow. The mourners'
lips are set, severe: a cartoon kind of pain

I am not fooled by two who share a single space – the sketch is by
another's hand, is not the one who burnishes a gold-leaf sky with silk
and canine tooth

Colours glow with names I relish: vermillion and dragon's
blood, malachite and azurite, saffron, verdigris and lapis – precious
lapis: blue of ancient light

Four seasons soaking into skin. This scribe has scratched
the parchment with his knife to try and scrape away mistake. There is
a hole and he has written round

WOMAN-TREE

(In Norse mythology the gods formed Ask and Embla, the first man and woman, out of driftwood.)

Look how they scuttle   the sea-louse   the gribble
appalled as the grain of my driftwood
stings into skin

I was Ash you were Elm in a wolf-
wind storm – broken and gashed, two
dull carcasses: witless, salted,
stripped.

I am heavy with limbs   a moon-bend of pain

Woman-tree touch my fingers, my face –
how fragile your syllables feel on my tongue:
Em-Bla ... a kiss
on my lips ...

I long for the forest
my bark and branches   the lift
of a wet-thin leaf

There were moments of water and sun –
now with the worm and the low-nest gull
we are rootless and hurt

An end to your riddles   your sour-fish dirge
I am wild for earth

TITANIA'S WOOD

Her snakes are enamel in moonlight, hot
and heavy as chains. They stir uneasily; hiss.
In her rosebud bower she twines love-knots
with ribbons as gifts for the child. Unnoticed
her husband paces the forest, plots how best
he can hurt his wife, take over and gain
control of the boy. They are both obsessed.
This is a poisonous wood – wolfsbane,
hemlock, a low-hanging moon in a pool
of frogs, pale-green and belly-up; dead.
The child sleeps on: as yet no unscrupulous
moonbeams disorder the curls on his head.
In sweet-briar dreams his world is kind –
later he'll learn not only worms are blind.

FACES OF FOX

Body like an arrow poised
in tension, heart's-
own aim

One who will not dance in daylight
fox-fur, fire-red
flame

Medieval beast
of chase you seek
forgotten woods

Quicksilver servant of the gods
disguised as fox
in woman's

skin, you cry
I am Seductress –
Come

GALILEO'S TIME

This balcony would love us.
We will have chairs in a white
wrought-iron, a table for books, jugs
of the best cold wine.

Tree-high and we will go skywards –
peer through a spyglass at moons and at stars
to find Galileo and mention that time
is passing for us
in the way it has passed
for him.

Who was it said if you paint a small cage
then later the bird will fly in?

Here is a balcony ready for two.
I will draw chairs, a table with books,
a jug and glasses for wine.

THAT THING

I am, as Shelley says, a spy for God and so
will seek this gristle out – the heart:
a seat of feeling and that thing
called love.

Of course they knew it
from the start, those wise Egyptians
with their scales: no out-of-kilter
tillers for Osiris and no pleas
for hues of grey. In the weighing
of the heart, black sheep
would go with goats –

as did Shelley, I suppose, the blackest
sheep in some men's eyes though
idolised by those who cared ... take
Trelawny on the beach, that grisly
pyre, the way he snatched the poet's
heart out of the flame. We read
how Mary kept the relic, had it
buried in her grave – a claim,
a lure for afterlife, to hook
her sweet fish in?

But why the heart and what
enigma is its symbol – target fit
for Cupid's arrows, woman's
buttocks or the vulva's lips?
I'm with Pliny that its shape's
the silphium – a plant once noted
as a purge for vicious humours (and
a contraceptive too) – Emperor Nero
we are told, obtained the final
precious stalk although Catullus
praised it to his Lesbia and he
that lyricist of love and lust
was bound to test its gift.

'SOFTLY, AS I LEAVE YOU'

She hurls herself from an empty bed –
his absence tangible
as rock

Outside
the island is nothing
but sand, nothing but moon

Vulnerable, she is
the addressee

of a corny sixties song

Yesterday's shadow
she will know
what it's like to remember

to be

more stone than a stone

And everything's ending in violet
dawn-light's a froth

egg-white

in a cracked
and trickling bowl

GLANCING AT LABELS

she sings the tune in a different key
and the rhythm is faster and quite
upbeat but the lyric's not new and
the theme's the same and it's
always that guy from an earlier
song who mattered and meant
a lot to her then though her life's
moved on and he is not in it and love
is a plaque high up on a wall that
tells how a person once living is
dead but the bricks exist and his
name's on a blue and white plate

so she scrapes some memories out
of the rubble as if they were trinkets
lost in the blitz and scribbles a phrase
of heartache and rain as pub
walls heave with calls for more
bitter and she winds good strings
on her old guitar though no one
will listen and glances at labels
on bottles of beer like *hop
garden gold* and *fiddler's elbow
spitfire* and *end of the world*

HEARTWOOD

Firescar   your death attacks
the pith of me

for your blue flame
like anthracite
is dull and cindered out

and I have pencilled
silence in   no music but
the crying slide

I wanted to be anchored at low tide
    bells across a quiet field
    two hares boxing in the mist

Enough of such
soft tissue dreams

Let weeds grow dark

There is still sap
in heartwood   fecundity
    in roots

GARNET FOR BIRTH

In January you bought me a birthstone ring.
I read how warriors going to battle
might, for luck, carry a garnet
to stop the losing of blood.

Such evocative names for a stone:
mandarin, pyrope, almandine –
for me they evoke Merovingian gold
and one sad queen who lies alone
in a Frankish tomb with a garnet ring
translucent as seeds of the bright
pomegranate – that fertile
abundant fruit...

Today the sky is nursery blue.
Garnets come in every shade, except for blue.
You mutter words of re-assurance
tuck my sheet in, squeeze my hand;
I rest the garnet on my belly,
pray it stops the blood.

AFTER SUNDAY

Look at you, priest in the car park,
offering palm leaves, bleached, to the men.

Where are you going
hound in the mist, rapid and thumping on snails?

Goose, you are flying too low; that river
is flat, the colour of lead.

And who is the person of alcoves and edges
who shouts like a placard at doors in the sky?

Tower-tall heavy bells echo
with footsteps, mottle in feathers and wind.

Mud in low fields is attentive and dark;
waits with the shelduck for rain.

HINTERLANDS

Hour-glass sands leap up in a storm,
hurtle us, god-like, to earth:
astral gold, we buffet the heavens and fall.

Quieter now: clouds thicken above the camp;
days are shorter; shadowed.
There is little sun.

There's a spot, they say, in the hinterlands
where we might dig for a tin-blue mineral,
patch up this rickety sky.

Shall we excavate an orchard? Scrape our nails in dirt?
We could tell our memories as if rosary beads,
say a *pater noster* to the air ...

... or maybe uncover an apple tree:
scrump for windfalls, feel the squash,
the under-footedness of them on grass.

SEURAT, IT'S A LONG SUNDAY

A child in white is looking at you,
if that's you by the canvas edge.
A crowded, Sunday, riverside scene
but the sound's turned off and nobody's
talking or kicking up needles under the pines –
they're not even looking at yachts.
It's a case of each in his solitary zone
with a drooping sun and a single cloud,
an overhang of moody, pensive green.

Well, leave them in their joyless profiles
and cross to the other side. Someone's
standing in the river, his voice is booming
through his hands. No? No good?
Sound muted here as well? Clouds
blend into a watery mist. How lethargic
and flabby they seem, these men
on their one day off.

You know the solution, don't you?
Go north. Away to the emptiness of the coast,
its long bare beaches, yellow-soft sand.
Un-people the lot of it. See what's left –
terrains of light, a stippled blue,
a post to tie up your own rowing boat,
anchors at twilight that hold.

THE NOT-YET LOST

entranced by dust
she patterns and swirls
a criss-cross of spirals
to see how the tiniest
touch of a finger-tip
alters the surface of grey

subtleties quiver
routes out of feathers
fibres of cotton
cells of her skin
wisps of a web
a butterfly's wing –

hooked on a quest
for grit and grime
she delves and probes
in cracks and creases
scrapes up fluff
from hut and palace
toenail clippings
of the famous, belly-
button floss

soon she's adept
at weaving and binding
her delicate, intricate
miniscule shapes
out of the debris'
bits of the not-
yet lost

It's the infra-thin
she says, the part
behind the shadow's
shade – a kind
of mapping for the
dust's discarded
and decaying
links: the bond
of us and us

A SUGGESTION OF LEAVES

Floating Worlds

A gardener washes lily leaves to clean away soot from the passing trains. He does this each morning before you get up although you are quite a lark yourself – an old, insomniac, half-blind lark, but still a bird of the dawn.

How terrible it is you say, the way light goes. You live in a new kind of duration, a matter of memory, doubling back. It is all hours and every season, floating, diffused. Losing the blue, you are seeing in russet and yellow, drifting further beyond the horizon, over the frame, the edge.

A Little Green Bridge

Moving in you lower the high walls round the grounds, gaze out. You enjoy selecting and planting seeds knowing these are the flowers you will paint. Soon you will grow Japanese cherry, crab and cider apple trees, arches of roses. You build a little green bridge.

View from a Train

It is early morning, clear in the valley, pastel warm. You glimpse this place. Here is a liquid element – a pool for the sun and a pool for the shade. There are colours under the water, movement of stems, reflected light.

The Speed of Sun

You work in a frenzy, following the hours from shadow-blue to burnt-orange sundown. It is more than the light. You would paint the air.

Frozen Roses

Whatever the weather you are there, on foot or by boat with your winter palette. Frost seeps through in violets and greys. The whole village is under snow though a hill in the distance has a lilac tip. The river is frozen for months. Each morning you wake to the sound of ice, melting, smashing.

A Palette of Diamonds

In the South there is a different light, subtle, un-nameable shades. Fairy air, you think. You talk about pomegranates, olives, dates, paint the swirl of the mistral, a vast sky, mountain, city, water. You are a man of wide open spaces, pure and pink and blue.

Limestone and Chalk

There are secret forces here you say as you dine on oysters and saffron soup and paint the green of sea, purple fields, a curved white road. Later you try to capture the battering winds. It is bleached and rugged. Rocks are ancient and strange.

The Parasol Years

In a studio boat you are closer to water. Here are regattas, bright young artists, families, friends, picnics on lawns and springtime through branches. You shimmer through it all – a tapestry time of poppies and sun.

A Suggestion of Leaves

You are starting out. A friend suggests you leave the studio, get into the open, the blue sky. The curve of a line acts as a river, a dab of ochre hints at a face. You are young and there is so much. You ask how your canvas can possibly show all those leaves.

A MESOLITHIC SLANT

He's on the cusp of revolution though he'll never know it –
any more than voles in the barley who'll breed a Scottish line.

All he can tell is that his world
(his scary and stinking-of-animal world)

is threatened by settlers who savage the pine
and turn wild boar into pig.

Just so does sunlight
shove its small beak through an earlier fog, lifting its face

to brightening air, like one who unwittingly
dines with an angel and cannot

be sure, for the rest of his life, if it's fear
or elation he's in.

RAVILIOUS ON THE BEACH

Here autumn waves are dun and rust
beneath a south wind sky. Backlit
the houses rise in tiers, the downs
are smoke in mist. Did you
see this? Your canvases reflect
the mood of it, a landscape stretching
far beyond the frame.

You don't reply. They said you always
were elusive: 'Boy' they called you
like a Peter Pan who's quite
intangible; a glow worm
on the evening lawn obscured
by light from lamp and room –
will you still toss your dark hair back
and walk away again?

Or are you closer to enigma
in those giant and grey-green hills,
the white of chalk scratched out
in thin-beat hooves?

FLANEUR WITH DOG

He wanders into a graveyard, enjoying
the sun on the back of his neck, a headstone's
lichen batik.

A gentle derive. He's aware of an elderly spaniel dog
following him into the town; hopes it isn't
directionless like him.

He enjoys this Tudor part of the street
with its magpie houses and tiny windows with faces
behind them that quiver like moons in a well.

They greet 'The Archer' on Tunsgate Hill:
his arrow, as always, points at un-seeable stars.

Twilight: the silting river brings in smells of fog.

A chipped and weathered set of steps
(a mounting block from towpath days)
stands at the edge of a lane.

The spaniel whines, sits down.
What? Can't you manage steps?
We're a pair with our tired old bones.

He stoops and cradles the dog in his arms:
You know what they say about stairs not there?
You'll meet yourself coming back.

Slowly the Archer steadies his bow, sights
his invisible star. There are shifts in the air.
Man and dog step up.

BROOD-WORM

I am considering footprints – all those tiny bones
that travel miles across the earth, connect
with clay, with other people's soil.

Heron flies over the dark-brown lake
wood pigeons cry out in tongues.
The brood-worm nestles and waits.

She is ancient, impartial, reveals
many wisdoms: a circle of chairs, hands
that touch for a while.

An old cat drinks from a fountain, later
sleeps in the sun. I notice the gold on a diligent
wasp, see others notice it too.

THE KELP DAYS

Later
came the running kind:
the sort whose springy limbs would over-
leap the drowning tide to sprint
on higher ground –

unlike the tribe
of wet-wool mammoths, swamped
and sunk in graves of sludge
as spring-time waters rose.

Compressed and lightly
traced in rock, a residue
of sedges, antlers, wormwood,
scallops, skinned and gutted
arctic foxes – strata of a scant
and arid world.

Beringia: a land of claws. You struggled
through the winter months when crabs

were frozen in their shells and pollock, hard
as flint, were beached; when any shadow

might be bear, and birch and alder
stripped by frost to less

than twigs, gave no protection
from the lash of wind.

Yet an outcrop might be shelter;
you had thick hides and wolverine fur
to warm your bed.

There were days
for gathering kelp
before the long walk on.

But it's light
I wanted to ask you about: its utter
whiteness, and if it was part of a seasonal
pattern, like the saiga's coat that turned in spring
from snow to cinnamon-brown ...

And if, some nights, you paused
in your trudging to notice how stars were so
close together there was almost
no space for the dark.

ARTICHOKES AND AN OLIVE GROVE

Your spirit slumps in the saddle.
Easier, you say, to look down not up
when your weary head like an over-blown poppy
droops on its stem.

But down is where all shadows meet,
where even the rays of a posthumous sun
fail in their glitter and reach.

What can I offer to make you look up?
A far-away island seeded with hope?
No, you reply, island is another word
for homesick, for small, torn edges of sand
where whale pods beach.

A small farm then, in the backhills?
Old Laertes lived there: cuttlebone-
flat in his moods. You too could hoe
around the vine, think back
to the naming of trees.

You are starting to un-slump.
In those hills is an olive grove
and a plot of land to grow artichokes on
where we shall put that donkey
out to graze.

STRANGE LOOP

White moon over a field of frost and a hare in icicle grass by a tree
stares at me in the low light

And I stare back at him into the light, forgetting the train
and my single bag – spider in amber, lion in tar - I cannot move.

Is it a riddle, a trick of the eye, a trio of hares where the brain is fooled
in the counting of ears –

where last is first and truth's a lie and I'm still here though life
goes on without me again as it always does

and this hare and I are caught in a loop of cold white light and nothing
is different, even if one of us shifts?

ALL THE INVISIBLES

Let's make a detour you'd say, find us
a ley-line or two. I was used to this: a sudden

appearance of all the invisibles, something
slanting or something blue, a lattice

of light through a leaded window as you,
my directional compass-rose, would sense

the silences moving the air: a man or horse
carved into grass, the last-rung bell of a church

gone under the sea. On quiet-hot days
with a feeling for tides, this was an island

that quivered with maps as we wandered
the way of the shell. Even droppings

of gulls on the shore or pebbles mottled
and bleached by salt were seen as offerings

meant as a token: private, intimate
gifts. So when did the music

of those silences turn to a canticle
scribed with a thorn? While I was looking

at runes in a feather, you fell in love
with the whiteness of chalk, the long, slow

curves of a pale-green land, a languorous
stretching of hills. And I am left

on a shingle beach with nothing but empty
spaces around me and nothing is moving the air.

IGNATIUS OF ANTIOCH LOOKS FOR STARS

They will know, our black-hole hunters, how it feels to sweep the skies
for particles of ancient stars that burgeoned in a molten fire
before this world was born.

You dreamed, they say, of anthems and of canticles,
of radiant cherubs with small wings who'd hum their sweet
harmonious parts in antiphons of song.

Was this your recompense for living on?
To be the final crying voice, the last disciple
when the rest were dead?

In the end were you a bone, wind-whitened on a dreary night
a snuffy-brown and slaty flute
inaudible, even then?

Now I hear they're bringing back Blake's vision-tree to Peckham Rye:
a sapling whose thin branches yet
may spangle in good stars.

AEOLIAN RAIN

Whole sky raining on bracken and mud
as water, untrammelled, tumbles with gusto
into the drought.

A not-yet flooded earth's
gulping for more as bubbles and weeds
rush over contours and edge.

Chaucer, is this what you mean by 'vertu'?
April showers, you say, pierce roots,
bathe every vein, each leaf ...

Is this the essence
of cabbage and rock,
the verb

'to become'
in a silver, lunar willow
or a sparrow with wet feathers in the hedge?

This wind is like iron on the plains of Troy
dying in an aftermath with a bloody sun.

Once there were four strong winds,
each with a name and puffed out cheeks

bombastic, overblown,
quartering the thermals of the globe.

Look at those horses –
eyeballs of Fool's Gold, hooves that would hit.

And always in pursuit
a family of breezes:

minor and quarrelsome,
wheezing along like bellows.

You say the wild turkey
will break

Its legs, too long and spindly for clay,
need an overlay of bronze

So you'll use a soft brush
to burnish its spurs, the wattle,
breast-feathers, snood

And I'm caught
by the metal – the shine of it all

which calls out to me like autumn and salt
from a world that is Baltic
and flint

I would share earth with you
waves of the soil

Otherwise

we become
flat-fish
length-wise cut, filleted
to the bone

    There's a Ringing Singing Tree in Burnley, Lancashire:
pipes of metal on another windy plain.

Like tombstones in Whitby, hunched above the bay,
the sculpture, on tiptoes, lowers its head to the wind.

Once, from a car, I saw the Angel:
colossal; revelatory; the skyline its voice.

Shelley would have loved the Singing Tree –
though he, who modulated air, would be the wind itself.

All the Invisibles
Mandy Pannett
SPM Publications, 2012
www.spmpublications.com
www.sentinelpoetry.org.uk/publications/alltheinvisibles